HOW TO WRITE AND PUBLISH NONFICTION BOOKS ON AMAZON THAT WILL SELL

A STEP-BY-STEP GUIDE

© Copyright 2021 Steve Pease - All rights reserved.

It is not legal to reproduce, duplicate, or transmit any part of this document in either electronic means or in printed format.
The information provided is truthful and consistent, in that any liability, in terms of inattention or otherwise, by any usage or abuse of any policies, processes, or directions contained within is the solitary and utter responsibility of the recipient reader.

Under no circumstances can any legal responsibility or blame held against the author for any reparation, damages, or monetary loss due to the information in this document, either direct or indirect. Respective authors own all copyrights. The information in this document is for informational purposes only and is universal as so.

All trademarks and brands within this book are for clarifying purposes only and are property of the owners themselves, not affiliated with this document.

TABLE OF CONTENTS

WHERE TO START
MAKE A TEMPLATE
PICKING A SUBJECT
PICKING THE KEYWORDS
PICKING A TITLE
RESEARCH
MAKE A MINDMAP
WRITE YOUR INTRODUCTION
BODY OF THE BOOK
CREATING A COVER
EDITING YOUR BOOK
FORMATTING YOUR BOOK
PUBLISHING YOUR BOOK
LAUNCHING YOUR BOOK
CREATE SPACE
CONCLUSION

WHERE TO START

So, you have written a book, or you have an idea for a book you think people would love to read. Now what? There are thousands of authors who have written books and published them on Amazon. Amazon pays out tens of millions of dollars every month to authors for royalties. From what I have read, over 50 % of authors on Amazon make less than $100 per year. The main reason is, they do not do a few things you need to do to sell books and make money.

Why is writing a book for Amazon a good idea?

There are several reasons it is a great idea.

- You can do it for free.
- Amazon is the biggest bookseller in the world.
- Selling books on Amazon is easy to manage.
- Amazon pays you nice royalties, and they do all the selling and delivery.
- The right books will keep on paying you for years.

The hard part is, there are a lot of things you need to do to get a book to market that will sell. You could do the research and figure out how to get your book written, and for sale like I did. But, if you do not know the best way to do it, you will compete with millions of books. This will make your chances of readers finding your book difficult. It will also take you a lot of time to learn all the tips.

I have read hundreds of books on publishing on Amazon. Many of them filled with great information about how to do it. I have taken all I have read and use and put together a system that works. It makes it easy for going through the writing process and getting it ready to publish. The information in this book will save you hundreds of hours.

Some techniques I have read about and tweaked them to fit what works for me. I am all about being as efficient as possible and that is what I wanted to create with this book. You can do your first book without all the trial and error. You will not have to keep redoing books to get them their best. Or you can read what works to get there quick.

I have put all the information into a detailed tutorial for each part of the process. This will show you how you can get your book ready fast. I go through each section in the process and tell you the best and easiest way to do it the first time.

You will learn:

- Why should you write a book?
- You will learn how to pick the subject.
- You will learn how to make a mind map.
- You will also learn how to make an outline.
- I will teach you to write an intro that will sell your book.
- You will learn how to write the main content of the book.
- You will learn to pick the best title.
- You will learn to create a cover that will sell.
- I will show you how to edit your book.
- You will learn to pick the best keywords.
- You will learn to get printed copies of your book.
- And you will learn how to never have a writer's block.

Like I said I spent four years and have read hundreds of books about how to get your books on

Amazon. I also have over 40 books for sale on Amazon. Once you get them on Amazon, then you need to know how to get people to buy them. I wrote for a few websites around 10 years ago, and I was having fun. I was even making a little money, but I wanted to reach more people.

When I found out about how anyone could write books and get them self-published on Amazon, I thought, that is cool. I took a subject I was passionate about and put together a book on it. [It is a complete how-to-book on playing disc golf](#).

I have been playing disc golf since 1978 and have been writing about it since 1995. I got the book together and put it on Amazon. I sold a couple of books the first month and 4 the next. It was not exciting. Then I read about how to do it, and I started selling more. I used what I learned and added more books. I now have 48 books for sale on Amazon. I have sold several thousand of the disc golf books alone. Many people still want a hard copy as well so do not ignore that market.

This has turned from a fun idea into what I dreamed it could be. I enjoy writing and sharing my knowledge with others. My goal is to be at 100 books by the end of 2020. I have updated and edited and changed the original disc golf book several times over the two years. That book is still my best seller.

Reading this book will help you get past the point you want to be without doing all the work I did. You can avoid all the reading, and trial and error I went through to get here. This can help you, so you do not have to redo your books many times. You should still edit them with updates occasionally, but you do not have to fix things if you do it right to start.

If you read this book and do the things from the book, you will get your books done faster. You will also not get stuck trying to decide what to write. You will not have to keep fixing your books, and you will not have to worry about if you wrote enough, or if you finished.

Why should you write a book?

Things have changed over the past several years. As far as what people are looking for when it comes to getting information. Because of how all our lives have changed, and everyone is always busy. People want their information in a specific article or book.

They want a book that solves the issue they are trying to fix without all the surrounding fluff.

There are things you know about that other people want to know about. You want to write it in a way so they can learn what you know in a simple format. Get them the knowledge quick and easy, and they will buy it. Your knowledge and experiences are valuable information. People want to learn what you know.

As an author, you want to address the problem and give them the solution in the quickest way possible. Explaining the solution so they can resolve the problem with your guidance. Books about specific issues are more sought after than a book that covers an entire subject.

A good example is photography books that cover one subject. If someone is looking forward to learning about photography. They want to learn how they can take better pictures. They will search for specific types of photography. A good book about photography will be specific about a particular type of photography. It will not give an overview of photography. It is too broad a subject to cover in a single book, and more information than a reader wants.

If you drill down into photography and write about a specific type. You will be more likely to cover what they want to learn in a shorter more concise package. The reader may want to learn about wildlife photography. They may want to learn only about bird photography. So, if you write a book about the best tips and techniques for taking great photos of birds, more people will buy it than if you are trying to sell a book of general photography.

This also allows you to write more books about photography that will sell to more people. You will reach the people that want to learn about specific forms of photography. The reader may want to learn how to take excellent portraits. Other readers may look forward to taking the best shots of pets or family members. Other readers may be looking forward to learning tips about photographing cars.

The possibilities are great of being able to write 10 books that cover specific types of photography. There are many photographic topics that the readers want to know about. Specific books will be much more sellable than a book about general photography.

This same thing will apply to any subject. Take the big subject and drill down to a specific subject that people want to learn about. Everything you know how to do. Everything you have knowledge about is also information other people want to know.

MAKE A TEMPLATE

Making a template for your books is a step that will save you a lot of time and work from the beginning. If you plan on writing more books, this is a big step. If you want to write and sell books, you want to write many books. My goal is to have 100 books for sale on Amazon. I have 48 books for sale at present. Because I enjoy writing and there are always more things people want to learn about, I will not likely stop at 100.

I have used several programs for writing. I started with Microsoft word. I tried Scrivener and Google Docs. I now do all my writing in Google docs. Because of how Microsoft word has changed in the new version, I have gone back to word as my main program for writing. Any program that works for you, and you like is fine.

I do still use Google docs for some of my writing. The best thing about it is that you can use it offline on almost any device. If I am going to the cabin or somewhere that I need to save space. I use my Chromebook. I can write on the Chromebook and open it in word because Google docs will download it for you as a word file.

Word works well. It has all the formatting and everything you need for writing. The downside of Microsoft Word is the limits on where you can use it. You need to do it online, or you need to have a windows computer with Word on it. The editing and formatting in word has gotten substantially better in the later versions. I signed up for the Microsoft 365 and pay a reasonable yearly cost to use it and it updates when they make changes.

Many writers rave about Scrivener. It is a nice program, and once you learn how to use the features, it works well. It has limits on how and where you can use it. If you write on one computer all the time, it is a good option. I learned great ideas from using it. Many of the ideas I use in Google Docs and in Word, I learned while working in scrivener.

The reason I do not like Scrivener as much, is that I write on several different computers. I have one in my office, one in my family room and a Chromebook that I take with me when I go out. Google Docs can work on the Chromebook on or offline. It also works in Windows on Chrome either online or offline. As soon as you get back online, it updates to the cloud. The program also saves all changes as soon as you make them when you are writing. Word also has an auto save mode now that I feel much better about. If I am writing offline, I also save a copy on a flash drive, so I do not have it only on the Chromebook.

If I write on the laptop in my family room, everything I do is on the cloud. If I write on my desktop in the office, everything is on the cloud right away. I can switch from the family room to the office or vice versa, and I do not have to take a copy on a flash drive. It is all updated everywhere right away. We have a cabin where we spend a lot of time during the summer, the Chromebook is perfect for that.

There is no Internet there. Because of the long battery life of the Chromebook, I can write for 8 to 10 hours without plugging in. That is another huge advantage of using the Chromebook. At the cabin, I save it on the computer and on the flash drive just in case it is lost. When I get home, it updates to the cloud, and I can access it anywhere again.

Google Docs and Word now have several other things I use that are very handy. There is a voice typing option you can use to talk while the program converts it to text. I have used Dragon software for this in the past, and I was not impressed with it. I do not use this way a lot, but it is nice sometimes.

Another thing I use for editing is an ad on called Pro Writing Aid. It has a small cost to get it, but it is invaluable when editing. You can check grammar. You can also check writing style and several other things. This will tighten your writing up and make it the best it can be.

Microsoft word also has great editing tools built into the program now that are extremely useful. The read aloud option is an invaluable tool when editing. It gives you a way to read with the program as it reads it out loud to you. That way you can see it and hear it at the same time to see if it sounds the best. It also has grammar checking and several other editing tools that I use all the time.

In Google Docs you can also have an outline set up on the left side of the screen while you are writing. It is easy to get to the part of your book you want to go to. On the right side, you can research without leaving the document writing screen. This is one thing Scrivener has that I liked.

Another part of Scrivener I liked is you can have each chapter separated while writing. Breaking the book into pieces makes it simpler. It is also less overwhelming when you do the re writing and editing. Looking at 2 to 10 pages feels much easier than looking at 100 pages.

Here is how I set up my template.
Set the text to Georgia font and the size to 12 points. Amazon uses Georgia when it converts for Kindle. I figure I would use it when writing the book. It is also a nice font to look at. I set the headers at size 18. I like to use a colored text for the headers for a different look. Use color, or not. It is my preference to use the colored text for chapter titles.

The first page is the Title page with the copyright notice. [Here is an article that has samples you can copy and use in your books](). Change to information to fit the year and your name, and you are all set.

Page 2 is the Table of Contents. When you set up your template, I would start with 10 chapters as a starting point. You can add or take away from this depending on what you need, but it is a good place to start. Type the header in the center on the page as Table of Contents. Next list Chapter 1 through 10 down the left side on the page.

TABLE OF CONTENTS

Chapter 1
Chapter 2
Chapter 3
Chapter 4
Chapter 5
Chapter 6
Chapter 7
Chapter 8
Chapter 9
Chapter 10

Change the line spacing of your chapter titles to fit the page best. This depends on how many chapters you have. Make it look good. When you use the template for a book, do not leave the Chapter and number on it. Change the chapter numbers to show the chapter title instead of Chapter number. Show the real chapter names for that book. You also want to have a link to each of the chapter titles. So, the reader can go to that chapter if they want to do that. I will go over how to do that later.

Page 3 is the Introduction or why should you read this book. This is where you sell the book to the reader. Tell them what problem they are facing, and what solution you offer. Tell them why they should listen to you and why they should buy the book. We will go over more on this later. We are making the template now.

You can change the header later also. Make it something that will get the reader to look at it so you can sell the book and tell them why they need to read it.

The next 10 pages are the Chapter pages. Type a header of Chapter 1 through chapter 10 at the top of each page. This is to give you a place to start. Change the header when you are writing the book.

The last section is the Conclusion or wrapping it up. Type a few paragraphs that review what the book covered in an abbreviated way. A statement that can work as a quick reference to the reader. Adding checklists, tables, and references as part of the book fit here. Add a section of other books they may want to read. When you have books on the same subject that cover different aspects of that subject.

There you have it. Now you have a template you can use to start any Nonfiction book you want to write. Save it in whatever software you want to use to write your books. When you start a new book, open the template, and save a copy right away to another place. Save it where you want to keep the book you are working on now.

The way I do this is. In Google Docs or in Microsoft word, I have a file with my template book. I start a new file for each book under the name for the book. Give it a working name.

Close the template and open the copy, change the copy name to the working name for your book.

PICKING A SUBJECT

Picking the subject and picking keywords gets done together. The searches for a good niche and keywords are the same process. As you find your keywords and look for a niche. Write the keywords or save them somehow so you will have them later. This chapter and the next go together. Read through both and do both at the same time.

The next step is to determine what your book will be about. Like I said before, the subject should be specific. There are whole books written about picking the right niche for your book. You need to decide what you want out of writing. You can go after the books that make the most money, or you can opt for the books you want to write. Because that is what you want. Otherwise, you can do both. Write what you are passionate about and pick a niche where you can still make money.

Most writers will want to do the last. Writing what you are passionate about is much easier and will be more rewarding to you. You can find the right balance. You can also study the subjects that make a lot of money. You can get passionate about those things to where you want to write about them.

What you want to think about when picking a topic for your book.

- What do I want to write about?
- What people want to read about?
- What is a specific problem or issue people want to know how to solve?
- What do I know about this subject?
- Is there enough information to research for a good solution?

The best way to start is to take out a notebook and make a list of all the things you have done for a job in your life. Break down each job into parts of the job that you did. You can write about specific parts of the job. Then make a list of hobbies and other things you like to do. Do not leave out anything. Take time and make the list as complete as you can.

Narrow down to one topic you want to start with. Save the list, this is your future writing list. Take the subject you chose and break it down into all the subcategories you can think of. Say you pick pets. Pet care is a huge area and one that sells well. People love their pets and spend a fortune on them every year.

Break down the main pet topic to everything you can think of.

Grooming
Exercise
Food
Toys
Dogs
Cats
Birds
Exotic pets
Etc.

Then see if you can narrow the subtopics to more exact ones. Take dogs and break it down to types of dogs. You could write a book on a specific dog and how to care for and raise that type of dog. If you have one, you can add personal experience and stories about your dog. Things that will add value from the book to the reader. This book will appeal to readers thinking about getting a dog and may want that type of dog. They may have gotten a puppy. They may have had one for a while and want to learn more about that dog.

Then you break it down to what you want the subject to be. Go to Amazon and go into the search bar on the left side. Click the drop-down box and scroll down to Kindle store and select that. Then type the subject you are searching for. As you type in the subject, look at the suggestions that Amazon is putting up below where you are typing. If you type in a dog breed, it will help you drill down deeper into the subject. This will also show you the biggest searches on Amazon for the subject you are seeking.

Finish typing a subject that looks interesting to check out. Keep searching only in the Kindle store. This will pull up books on the subject you are looking for. What you want to look for is several books on the page that have a Best seller ranking of 50,000 or less. This is under product details a few inches farther down the page. The ranking is on the bottom section of the product details. A book in the 50,000 ranking is selling three or four books a day on average. This is a good place to start. This is a place you can get on the first page and get exposure to your book.

When you find a topic and find a specific niche that you want to write about, you are ready to start.

Here is a list of the top 100 niche categories on Amazon kindle books. These will vary, but for the past several years, these have all been hot topics.

Each of these top niches comprise several popular sub niches. Dig in and find the right one for you.

1. ADHD-- dealing with and treating
2. Acne-- reduce or get rid of
3. Adult Coloring Books-- This is big now
4. Alzheimer's--- Treatment, coping, everything about it
5. Anger Management-- Controlling, dealing with someone with anger issues
6. Anti-Aging-- All aspects of slowing the aging process
7. Antiques-- Pricing, selling, etc. all aspects of antiques
8. Anxiety-- Reducing and dealing with anxiety
9. Archaeology
10. Arthritis
11. Asthma
12. Astronomy
13. Back Pain
14. Backpacking
15. Bass Fishing
16. Become A Nurse
17. Bird Training
18. Boating & Sailing
19. Bowling
20. Boxing
21. Camping and Hiking

22. Cheerleading
23. Chess
24. Children's books -- Huge niche right now, picture books
25. Chronic Fatigue
26. Classic Cars
27. Cooking/Recipes
28. Copywriting
29. Decorating
30. Depression
31. Diabetes
32. Divorce
33. Dog Training
34. Drop-shipping
35. Eating Disorders
36. Gambling
37. Gardening
38. Get Your Ex Back
39. Golf
40. Greenhouses
41. Hair Loss
42. Headaches
43. Heart Disease
44. Hemorrhoids
45. Hiking
46. Honeymoons
47. Horse Racing
48. Horse Training

49. Hypnosis
50. Hypoglycemia
51. Insurance
52. Interior Design
53. Investing in Gold
54. Kindle
55. Lawn Care
56. Learn French, German, Italian, etc.
57. Learn to Dance
58. Learn to play Guitar
59. Learn to Sing
60. Life Coaching
61. Low-Fat Recipes
62. Magic Tricks
63. Marriage Advice
64. Massage
65. Memory Improvement
66. Menopause
67. Mental Health
68. Motherhood
69. Motivation
70. Mountain Biking
71. Multiple Sclerosis
72. Obsessive Compulsive Disorder
73. Organic Food
74. Parenting
75. Photography
76. Poker

77. Pottery
78. Pregnancy
79. Psychic
80. where to find free stuff online
81. Relationships/Dating
82. Romance
83. Running
84. Scrapbooking
85. Scuba Diving & Snorkeling
86. Self-Sustainability
87. Single Parenting
88. Skiing & Snowboarding
89. Stop Smoking
90. Stop Snoring
91. Swimming
92. Tattoo Removal
93. Time Management
94. UFOs
95. Wedding Planning
96. Wedding Speeches
97. Weight Loss
98. Weight Training
99. Wine and beer making
100. Woodworking

Here is how to dig in and break them down to find a good sub niche. Where you can compete and get to the top of the page where you will get seen. Take the last one on the list, Woodworking.

Woodworking main niche

Cabinet making--kitchen cabinets— cabinet joints— cabinet plans
Furniture making--table making— shaker style tables— joints for shaker tables
Outdoor furniture-- outdoor furniture for kids

You can keep breaking it down and go to different categories of woodworking. Look at every other hot niche.

PICKING KEYWORDS

The purpose of keywords is to help readers find your book. The key to good keywords is to have keywords in your title, subtitle, and your keyword lists. Do not make your title and subtitle keywords that do not fit. Do not stuff keywords and add them to get them in. The goal is to get your book on the first page for the Amazon search for the most keywords that pertain to your book.

What you need to do is find out what words people are using to search to find books that your book is about. There are a few good ways to do this.

The first is to use Amazon itself to see what people are searching for.
- Go to the Amazon website and go to the search box at the top of the page.
- In the search bar click in the drop box on the far-left side of the search box.
- Scroll down to Kindle Store and click on that, this makes it show only books.
- Type in the main subject of your book. Enter exercise as an example. The search will pull

up the main topics under exercise in a drop down below the search bar.

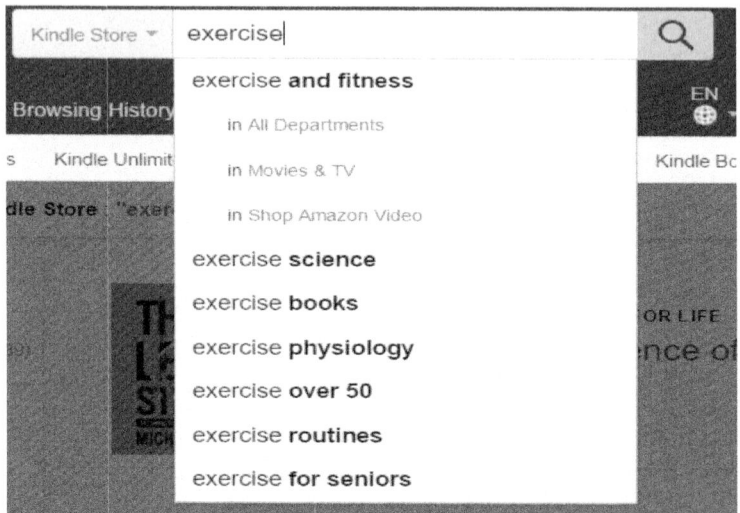

These are the top searches under exercise for books on Amazon. This is also a great way to find a niche for your book. Do not pick keywords because they are popular, make sure they pertain to the subject of your book.

If your book is about exercise as you get older, good keywords would be seniors, over 50. Then you can drill down deeper and get more. Type in seniors.

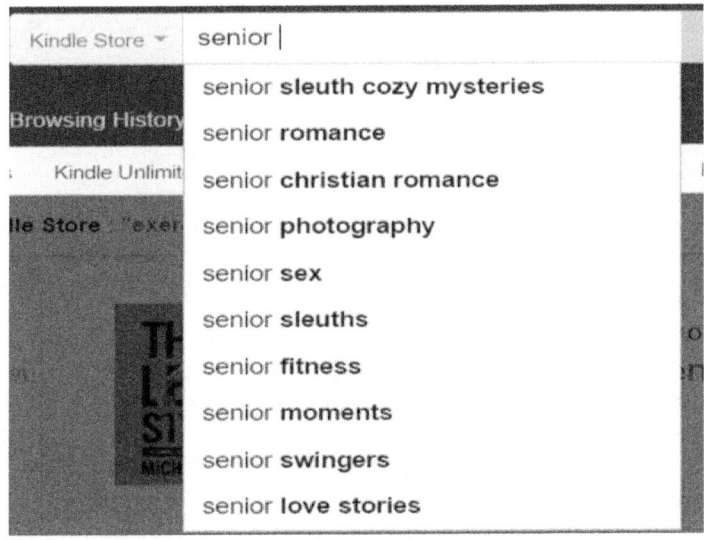

Now you get more things you know people are searching for on Amazon. Use any other keywords in the list that fit the book you are doing. Keep doing this for other subject words you think people may use to search for what you are writing about. Make a list of the keywords you want to use. Get as many as you can and give them a rating on how high they ranked and how well you think they will work.

The second good way to search for keywords is to use Google AdWords. This is a site you must set up an account and log into, but there is no cost.

Here is the link to the site.

- Sign in or create an account. If you have a Google account already, you can sign in with the same username and password.
- Click on the search for new keywords line. You can enter a word, a phrase. Or a group of words or phrases. You can change the search parameters below or not, and then hit get ideas.
- Look at the average number of monthly searches. The more searches the better for keywords. That means that more people are searching for that word or phrase. In the competition heading is where it shows how the competition is for advertising in that area. This means that if you look for exercise. And you go to the data. You see 100,000 to 1 million searches. This is good for a broad keyword but not specific to your category.

Experiment with this and find the best keywords you can for the specific topic you are writing about. So, if your book is about exercising as you get older.

Exercise is a good keyword to put in the title or subtitle. as well in the keyword list, but you only have seven keywords, or keyword phrases, to use in your keyword list. If a reader searches for exercise, they will never see your book with that keyword only. There are so many books under exercise you will not be able to get to the first page.

Use AdWords to find keywords. Play with it and search different phrases and words. Find the best ones to get the readers to find your book when they are searching for your subject.

If the reader searches for exercise for seniors. They will get a more specific list, and you will have a better chance of being on that first page. This takes some tweaking. I have changed keywords on some of my books, and it can make a big difference in sales.

There are other programs that will help you find keywords for your book. They will all help you find keywords. You can check them out and try them. Some are free. Some cost money. With a little work, you can do it yourself for no cost. Whatever you do, do not skip this part, or think it does not matter. This is the main way that readers will find your book. There are millions of books to choose from. If you rely on people to find your book by chance, your sales will be low, no matter how good your book is.

PICKING A TITLE

The title is another huge part of getting your book seen and selling it. The title and the subtitle need to leave the reader feeling like they must check it out. They need to want to find what this book is all about. To do that there are a few things you need to do.

Is the title memorable? Will the reader stop and think they need to know more, or will they go on to the next book title?

Does it create curiosity? Will they stop to think about your title, are they thinking it is interesting? Does it make them think, what does that mean? Does it make them say that is what I am looking for? You need to make them want to investigate more to see what it is all about.

What is in it for me? The key job of the title is to draw the reader in and hook them. The title needs to answer, what is this book going to do for me? What is the benefit to the reader if they look deeper into this book?

Would the reader feel embarrassed if their friends or family saw the title to the book they were reading? You may think this is not significant, but it is. People may not want others to see what they are looking for. They may be looking for information about an embarrassing problem. Or a personal problem they do not want to share. Your book may cover a touchy subject that could embarrass the reader. Take that into consideration when writing the title.

Does the title promise to solve the problem that the reader is looking forward to fixing? Do not make a cute or artsy title that the reader will not be able to tell what the book is about.

This is like when you are starting a business. One of the main things the name on a business should do is tell the public what the business does. I see many new businesses on the side of the road, or names on their vehicles. If customers see the name of your business, and they do not know what you do, you are losing a ton of business.

There is no reason for me to seek what that business does. There are plenty of businesses that tell what they do in the name on the business. If I must guess or research to find out, what do you think the chances are I will look deeper?

Make the title be obvious what the book is about. What problem it solves and what benefit is in it for them from reading your book.

Come up with 5 to 10 titles you could use in your book that do the things listed above. There is a website, I found that is a good place to get starting titles. It is for blog article titles, but it works for books as well.

I like to experiment with it when I get my title lists. The website is called **headline analyzer**. Type in your headlines one at a time and see, which gets the highest score. Work on the top couple of headlines and change and tweak a few things and see if you can get the score higher. It will at least make you think about the titles and see if you can make it better.

The site above is not the final say. It is a tool you can use to get the best title for your book. What it does is give you an idea of what works and how you can make it better. Anything that makes your book more attractive and more interesting will help sales. These are all ideas that will attract potential readers that are checking out books.

RESEARCH

I do my research on an ongoing basis. I use a program called OneNote. I read things every day on Facebook and news sites etc., and I also have Google alerts set up for specific topics. The alerts are set up for things I want to see the latest information about. Google alerts is a great research tool. You can set up as many as you want on subjects that you are interested in, and have it email it to you every day. I read the Google alerts and any articles I find that are worth keeping for future knowledge. I clip the article to OneNote and save as a file for later.

Google alerts are a key to getting and keeping up on the topics you want to follow. This sends you an email daily with important articles about the topics you set up. I have 20 Google alerts set up for a variety of subjects. Some of them get no new articles for several days. Some get up to 20 per day. It depends on what the subject is and how active it is.

Use Google alerts.
Go to Google and type in alerts. Then follow the setup for the subject you want to follow. Be specific on the articles you want to see. If you are too broad

on the subject, you will get too many articles to look at.

When I start to write a new book, I go to OneNote and set up a notebook on the subject the book is about. Then I go through the articles and look for articles that will fit my book. I put them into a stack in notebooks I separate into the chapters the book contains.

I also read a lot of books from Amazon and highlight meaningful segments as I read them. I look through the books about the subject and copy them to a new note in OneNote that I save for when I am writing the book. When I have researched all parts of the subject. I go to the next step for now and make a mind map for the book. You should read a couple of the top sellers in your niche before you even start to write to get ideas.

Research also includes writing down personal experiences that you have had. If you know other people that have knowledge about the subject, they may have useful stories and experiences that you can use as well. Other stories that you know that relate to the subject the book is covering are also useful.

Research is also any other gathering of information that will help you write your book. It can be interviews or meeting with people who know a lot about the subject. Look for ways that can help you in any way get more information on the subject that will be valuable for the reader. Make your book appeal to the people who will want to buy it. Give the information to solve the problem while putting your own twist and spin on it. Make it different or easier to solve the problem.

Another important step in deciding what to put into your book, is to go to the Amazon website and look at the top-selling books in your niche. Look inside and look at their table of contents. Look at the chapter heading that they use. What is included in their book? What are they leaving out that you feel should be in the book? These are 2 important things to ask yourself when putting your book together.

Then read the reviews of the books. Read the good and bad ones. Take note of what the readers like about the books and what they do not like. Use that information when you are deciding what to put in your book.

Make a list of stories that you have experienced. as well as stories you have read that would help the reader understand your points. Anything related to the information to help the reader solve the problem they are trying to solve.

When writing information books, use stories to break up the information and make the book more interesting to the readers. There is a tendency to get out the information as fast as possible. This is ok in some situations but adding a story or a good quote will make the reading more enjoyable for the reader.

If you do your research, and you have too much material for the subject. Tweak the subject down into more specific topics. Put together a series of books on each part of the subject you are covering. Writing a series of related books is the number-one way to get more sales on your books. If you write a good book, people will buy the connected books as well.

MINDMAPPING

The mind mapping gets done at the same time as the main research phase of the book. Do not skip this part, this will make your book much easier to write when you start. The mind map will have the whole book laid out ahead of time. You will never be at a loss for what to write about. The only thing you must do when you write it is to write.

If you do a mind map of your book, you will never have an issue with the so-called writer's block. You will always know what to write and what you still need to write. I often jump between chapters when I write. Therefore, setting up your template that has the chapters open is so important. You can easily write about one part, then skip to a different part if you have a good idea or read an interesting article that fits into another part of the book. You do not have to write the book in the order of the chapters. It all depends on what part of the research you are doing. This is another part of Scrivener that I took their idea from.

There are a lot of mind map programs out there. I use a program called Coggle and one called Xmind. You may like a different one better, whichever one works for you. I use these programs because I like the way they work, and they are easy to figure out. You can also save it and send a copy to another program or print it out, which fits into the way I write the books.

When you do the mind mapping, start with the main subject for the book in the center. Add on each chapter to the center subject. From there you go into each chapter and put together the points you want to make in each chapter.
Mind mapping is a type of outlining that helps you write the book.

Main subject-----------chapter title--------------point 1

Point 2

Point 3

Point 4

Point 5

It will look something like this. Do each chapter and the subheadings under the chapters. Take some time on this. The mind map is like the skeleton or the frame of your book. This is the new way to outline, and it is easier than a written outline. Everything you add to the book will fit into the chapters and subheadings. Once you get this part done, writing the book is filling in the spaces you have determined for the book.

Here is the xmind copy of another book I wrote. This is an amazingly simple one, but it shows you how to do it. You then add ideas and subgroups under the main ones in the mind map. I do sometimes add or take away from the original mind map. Most of the time when I get to this point, this is what the final book will look like in a graphical form. A lot of writers make an outline in the old style of writing.

This is much easier, and you can see the whole thing at one time. You can also change the order of the parts of the book by dragging a chapter to a different location. Then add the subjects you want to put into each main heading. Example: Under History, you can add. Start of piracy, reason for the start, British pirates, French pirates. Cover each part of that topic in the chapter, then move on to next.

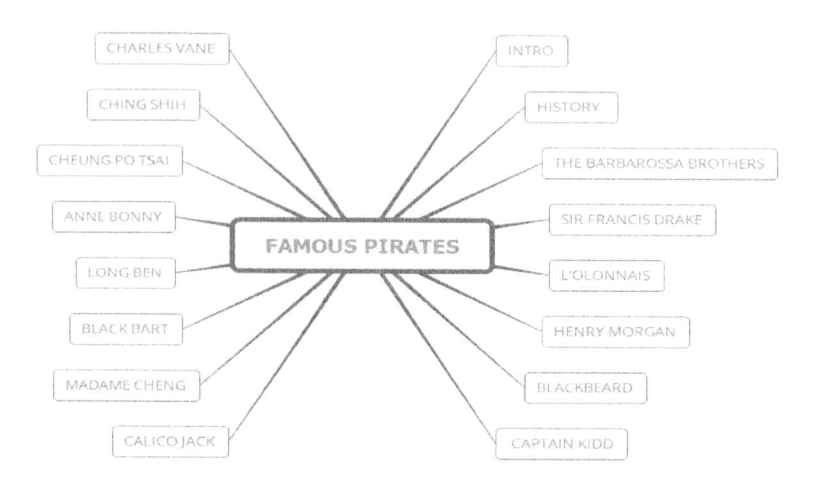

```
                CHARLES VANE                    INTRO
          CHING SHIH                          HISTORY
       CHEUNG PO TSAI                            THE BARBAROSSA BROTHERS
         ANNE BONNY                           SIR FRANCIS DRAKE
                          FAMOUS PIRATES
          LONG BEN                              L'OLONNAIS
          BLACK BART                          HENRY MORGAN
        MADAME CHENG                          BLACKBEARD
            CALICO JACK                       CAPTAIN KIDD
```

Do the mind mapping as you are doing the initial research so you can add in all the chapters you think the book needs. Some of the chapters you will decide you do not need; some you will decide you can combine with another chapter. This is where you do the changes so when you are ready to write, you are prepared to go at its full speed.

WRITE YOUR INTRO

The introduction is your sale letter. It must be good to draw the reader in and make them keep reading. The first line of your introduction should be a line that hooks the reader. Why should they read this book? Show them how to do something important. Teach them to learn how to _____. Tell them something to make them keep reading. I know from my personal reading if the author makes the introduction all about them, I lose interest in a hurry. Make the introduction about the reader and how they will benefit.

I have seen several introductions where the author starts by telling you who they are and why they wrote the book. Readers do not care at the beginning about you or why you wrote the book. They care whether the information will benefit them and teach them how to fix the problem.

You do not have to write the introduction at the beginning. Sometimes I do. Other times I wait until I finish the rest of the book. Most of the time I write it at the beginning, and then I add to it and update it after I finish the book.

This is the way you sell your book to potential readers. There is an eight-step process to writing a great introduction. Change the name to something other than introduction if you can. I like to use a header of where to start, or how to start, or something along those lines that will get the reader to read it. Introduction does not draw them in.

The 8 steps are easy, if you follow the steps. You will have a great intro to get the reader to read this part of the book and get them to act.

Step 1. State the problem that the books written to solve. Go into what the problem is. Why it is a problem? Can they relate to having the problem and wanting to have a solution to the problem? They found the book because of the title and the keywords for the book. We can assume that they are looking for a way to fix this problem. Sell them on the fact you understand and can relate to the problem, and you can help fix it.

Step 2. Step 2 will tell them the solution you have come up with to fix the problem they want to fix. Explain what the book will show them. And that when they finish the book, they will have the answer to what they are trying to fix. Use personal experience and examples of how what you are saying works and fixes the problem. Use examples and stories throughout the introduction. This adds to the value and authenticity of what you are saying.

Step 3. Step 3 is where you tell them why they should believe what you are saying. What experience have you had. What job have you done that makes you an expert on the issue and why you have the answer to the problem.

Step 4. Tell the reader and show the reader by example why they should read the book. How will they enjoy your book? Go over any benefits that will come to them from the information you are about to share with them.

Step 5. Amazon gives you plenty of space here to do what you need to do. Enter plenty of information to get the readers excited to see what the book has to offer in full. Use embellishment on the benefits. Use examples of how the advice benefited others or even yourself. Make it compelling to them to keep reading and wanting to buy the book to get all the information.

Step 6. Make a promise about what they can expect when they read the book and follow your advice or tips. Make the promise as big as you can deliver, but never write you can deliver something that the book does not offer.

Step 7. Warn them what they will miss out on if they do not get this book. You do not want to seem pushy here. What you want to do is to create enough interest in getting the solution to a problem they do not know how to fix. They will buy the book to get it fixed.

Step 8. The final step for the introduction is to tell them to scroll up and get a copy now. Encourage them so they do not forget and can have the solution right now if they get the book. Tell the reader to get the book now.

If you cover these eight steps in the intro. You will cover almost every question or objection that the reader could have about the book.

BODY OF THE BOOK

The body of the book is the meat. This is where the reader is looking for the answer to the question, or the solution to the problem. This is where you need to have the valuable information. The information needs to be easy to understand and simple for the reader to put in place. This is where you give the reader what they need.

When I start the writing process, this is how I set this up.

Start a folder in Google Docs or Microsoft Word called books working on now. Inside that folder create a file with the working name of the book you are working on. I sometimes work on more than one book at a time, so I keep them in this main file of Books Working on Now.

Inside the file for the book, I am working on has a copy of the template. Set up a separate file for each chapter of the book. This is a feature I learned from Scrivener I liked and wanted to use it in Google Docs. This way, you can work on whatever chapter you want when you are reading and researching the book. There are sometimes when you want to add something to more than one chapter. It is easy to switch between chapters when you are writing.

It also makes it simpler when you are doing your editing and future drafts of the book. It feels easier to edit a few pages at a time than the entire book. I will go more into editing in future chapters but trust me. This is much easier.

 A second huge advantage to Google Docs and Word is as you write the auto save changes every change you make right away. The program saves your work for you as you are typing or talking. You do not have to worry about something happening and losing what you were writing. Not all other writing programs do this. Google Docs now has a speech to text tool in the program that works great. I Sometimes use this feature. It works better than Dragon Naturally speaking program, and it is free. It gives you a way to write like you were talking to another person. Tell them the information as if you were talking to a friend.

When you get to this step and start writing the book. Look at your research articles and books and pick a place to start. The reason I like to set it up this way is now I can write the parts of the book I want to write, and in the order, I want to do them.

You can put it into the template in the right order when you are done writing.

As your writing the chapters, add things that make the information more interesting. Add things like anecdotes, personal experiences, and stories that illustrate the points you are trying to get across. Many people learn and remember things better if they have a story. Something to associate with the point you are making. Adding quotes from famous people helps readers remember. The information will stick better about the subject you are covering. It gives the reader more than one way to tie the information together.

Pictures are also great if they help add to the book and add to the learning process of the reader. Google Docs and Word make it easy to add pictures to your book. Make sure any pictures you add are your pictures, or you have the license to use them. Do not get too crazy with the pictures unless the book is a book that the pictures are a key part of the book. Because of the size of the pictures, the book will cost more to produce.

I have written a couple of books on photography. Those books will need more pictures to get the readers to see and understand the points. There are higher costs involved in having lots of pictures.

Amazon charges a fee per download depending on the size of the file. The more pictures and the larger the file, the bigger the download charge. You will end up making less or charging more to cover the added expense. If you need pictures, use them, it will cost a little more for the download fee. You will need to charge a higher price for the book to make the same royalties.

Most non-fiction books that people want now are to cover a specific part of a topic. Readers want to get the information they are looking for in the shortest time possible. You want to have your book educate the reader on all the pertinent information. Solve the problem you are covering in 8,000 to 15,000 words. This will make your book have 40 to 100 pages. This is a good size to get the information the reader wants and get it quick. They can read it in one sitting and learn the solution.

At the beginning of each chapter in the book, do a little introduction about the chapter. After you write the chapter, put a paragraph at the end of the chapter that is a wrap up for the chapter. Lists the action steps to take to do what is in that chapter.

Some readers skim and read only this part. If you have it, they will read it and then read the details inside. If you do not have it, they may skip the chapter and may even skip the book.

Try to write nonfiction books in the same way you would talk to a friend. Make it easy to read and tell them the information you are giving them. You can use your phone and use the voice to text option in the notes and go through the ideas in exactly that way. Talk to your phone and it will print the information out for you. Doing this will allow you to write whenever you get an idea about something to add to the book. You can copy and paste it into the chapter you want it in. I do this sometimes. It works well for lots of people, not so much for others. Try it, it may be the ticket for you.

Chapter Structure
Brief intro of what is in the chapter.
Step by step, on how to fix the problem.
Action steps that will help or follow the step-by-step process.

Depending on the information, you can make the whole book a series of stories that cover the points in each chapter. This works for some things but not all.

Do not use big words or tech jargon. Keep it simple and easy to read and understand. Write like you would talk, the way you would tell a friend the information. Write at a level that anyone can read and understand the solution to the problem.

CREATING A COVER

There are thousands of options in design for a cover. Having a good cover is one of the most important parts of your book. Do not think of this as an afterthought. Millions of people are looking for books and searching Amazon to find books. The way they look at a book or not is the cover and the title of the book. If you see two books on the same subject, one has a cool cover. The other is plain and boring. You will look at the book with the cool-looking cover and pass on the boring one.

You need a good title, an intriguing description, and a cool-looking cover. This will lead the reader to check out the good-looking book. They will buy that book and never even look at the other books. The cover, title and description are the sales tools for your book. This is your 30-second chance to get the reader to look deeper. Next, they read the title, and the title needs to grab them. The introduction is where you can tell them your book will solve their problem and do it quick. Show them the benefit to reading your book. Show them what is in it for me? That is all they are looking for.

People do judge a book by its cover. It may not be a good idea, but it is a reality. Having an attractive cover that makes the reader investigate is important. Each part of getting them to buy your book is all about selling the reader the benefits to them for reading your book. The cover, the title and the introduction are your sales pitch.

The picture you use for your cover should make the reader want to see more. It shows what they want to get from the book, or triggers an emotion for what they want to get from the book. [Here is a link to a random page](#) that used emotion to get people to look deeper. The book is about muscle building. If you want to build muscle, and you see what you want as your goal, it is more enticing. See what you think. Which books would you look further at? If the cover shows what you want, it makes it more appealing to the reader.

This book is a big seller. It has thousands of good reviews and is under 8,000 in sales of all books on the Amazon site. This author is making good money from this book. It is clear what problem the book is solving and the benefits of getting the book. It is available in all the formats so readers can get it in any form they want.

The best way to learn what people want, is to look at the top-selling books in the niche you are writing for. Study the covers and see what people buy. Model your cover after something working for others. Do not copy, use the ideas or style.

You can create your own cover or have someone do it for you. There are places like Fiverr that many people say is great. I have tried it twice and was not at all impressed by the outcome. I do not feel I got anything better, or not as good as I can do myself. I feel you get what you pay for, and Fiverr is low cost.

I have spent a lot of time looking at top selling books and their covers. If I see book covers, I like, I will save them in a OneNote file and look at them and use ideas from the designs I like. You can create your own covers if you use ideas from other top designs.

There is a program I use to create my covers that is great. There is a cost to the service, but you can make unlimited covers during the year. The program is easy to use, and you can create professional-quality covers on your own.

The program is **mycovermaker.com**. Check it out if you want to make your own covers. If you do not want to make your own, try Fiverr and see what you can get. It is inexpensive to try, and you could get someone great.

I am a photographer and have been for over 40 years. I have had extensive use of photo processing software over the years, with lots of experience in that area. If you have that talent, use it. If not, there are other places you can get covers. Yet, the cost is something you will have to consider as part of the book expenses. This is an important part of selling your book. You can pen the greatest book on the subject ever written, but if nobody looks at it. Of the millions of books on Amazon, it will not sell.

The cover is important. I also have an account with [Adobe stock](#) for pictures I can use in my books. I use many of my own shots, but I do not have pictures of everything I want a picture of. The Adobe stock subscription gives me photos for a cost per month. If you do not use them, they roll over to the next month, so it is one price for each for the choice of millions of good stock photos.

Use links in your book to give added value and other important information. You can link to articles. You can link to videos on YouTube, or you can link to other places in your book. Even other articles that cover the subject you are mentioning.

Put in links to important information, like the link above to Adobe Stock. Links that you add give valuable information about the subject and give the reader more information on fixing the problem, Links are valuable information to the reader.

EDITING YOUR BOOK

Most people will tell you to pay an editor to edit your book for you. You can do that, but with the right knowledge, you can do it yourself and do it well enough to make it work. A professional editor will cost several hundred dollars or more. If you will edit your book yourself, there are things you must do.

You must get all the typos and bad grammar out of the book before you finish the publishing.

There are several tools you can use to get it right.

- The first tool to use is the spell checker in your writing software. Microsoft Word has incredibly good editing built into the program now.
- The second tool I use is a piece of software that is online, or you can get a downloadable version for a small cost. The program called **Hemingway editor.** I am using it as I type this. This will show you sentence structure and overuse of types of words. It will give

you a great way to edit your book. While reading through the book. At the same time, you are making the words easy to read and easy to understand. Try the free version and see what it shows. It is not 100% correct. But it will give you something to go by and clean up your book so it will be easier and more enjoyable for the reader. No matter what the subject, you want to write the book at a level easy to read and understand.
- Another tool I have used is a program called White smoke. They keep improving this program.
- Another tool I use is Pro writing aid. This is an add on that is part of the tools you can get with Google Docs. There are many things you can check to improve your book with Pro writing aid.

1. Writing style
2. Grammar
3. Overused words
4. Consistency
5. Acronyms
6. Cliches

There are several more reports. The ones I use most are the Writing style, Grammar, and overused words. Try the different tools and see which one's work best for you.

- The next edit I do is have Microsoft Word read the book while I read it on the screen. If you have a kindle, you can email the document to the kindle and go through it on the kindle and have it read it to you as well. Look for things that do not sound correct. Look for misspelled words or words that the spelling is right, but it is not the right word for the text you are using.
- For example. You may have typed the word not when you should have typed the work knot. Or right and write. They are both spelled right but have different meanings. You may also have typed so when the word should be to. The spelling is right, but it is a mistake that the spell checker will not catch.

After you read through the book two more times, you should have all the mistakes fixed. You are now ready to format and publish your book.

After I have done all the editing and fixing on the chapters. Then I take them and copy and paste them into the template. It is easier to edit and add when it is only a chapter and not the whole long document.

FORMATTING YOUR BOOK

This part is important to make sure your book looks good when the reader downloads the book to read it.

Set up the order of the chapters. This may have changed some since the original setup, but it is easy to do. Copy and paste all the chapters together in the right order.

One thing that makes the book feel sloppy or not professional is having the book chapters not starting from the top of a page. Having the chapter start in the middle of a page looks bad. Make sure you get a page break at the end of every chapter so the next chapter will always start on a new page.

You also want to make sure you put a bookmark at the start of each chapter. Then put a link on the chapter titles to the bookmark. This way, the reader can click on the chapter title in the table of contents and go right to the chapter if they want to.

Go to the page setup and set the margins to 1" all around and the page size to 8 ½ x 11". When you upload the edited file to the KDP site, the final formatting will be set for the Kindle reader.

Download the program from Amazon Kindle called Kindle previewer. You can get the book all set up and formatted so it looks perfect before you upload it to the site to have it published.

Use the font Georgia and set the normal text to 12 points. This is what Amazon recommends. You can use other fonts, but this is what they say looks best on Kindle, and they should know.

PUBLISHING YOUR BOOK

When you're ready to publish your book, sign into your KDP account and log into your account. [Here is the link to the page.](#) When you get there read the tutorials that look like something you want to know. You can skip the things you know, but they will help make sure you understand what you are doing.

- Select create a new title. When you click on that page it takes you to where you input the book info.
- Select the language.
- Put in your title and subtitle how you want it to appear.
- Next you can enter your series number. Writing books in series is a great way to add extra sales. People will buy the next book if they like the one they read.
- Next you can add an edition number. If you rewrite or add a significant amount of new information to the book. Call it the second edition, or whatever edition it is.

- Next you enter the author information. And any other contributors and what their role was in the book.
- The next section is for the description. This is particularly important; this is your sales pitch to get the reader to investigate the book further. Use the tips in the chapter to write a killer description for your book.
- Then you state you own the publishing rights to the content. You wrote the book. Do not copy and paste from the internet other than a quote now and then. Make sure you wrote the material.
- Next is where you enter the 7 keywords you came up with. The words you feel will get the most readers to see your book when they search. Another key part to not take for granted. Research this part and make sure they are good; you only get seven.
- If your book is age restricted for content, put that in the next box.
- Hit the save and next button and go to page 2.
- Read the DRM info and decide if you want it or not.
- Then upload your saved formatted book to the server.
- Upload your cover to the server.

- Click on the kindle book preview and go through the book. Make sure that everything looks good and the way you want it to look. Make sure all the chapters are starting on their specific page. Look for anything you may have missed in the formatting step. This is what readers will see so make sure it looks good. If there are changes needed, go to your file, and change them. Then upload the fixed file and go through the previewer again and make sure it is right.
- When you are satisfied it looks good, hit the save and continue button and go to the next page.
- On the next page select if you want to be in the KDP select or not. If you are starting out, I would enroll in it. What it states you cannot sell a digital version of your book anywhere else but on Amazon for 90 days. You will be re enrolled if you do not opt out. Once you get more adept and want to branch out. You can opt out and sell your books everywhere if you want. This only affects the digital form of your book. I still have all my books enrolled. Read the info on what enrolling gives you and what it requires you to do. You also get to list your book for free for 5 days inside the 90 days, in whatever combinations you want.

You will see different recommendations on this. I launch my book for free for 3 days and save the other 2 for some time later in the 90-day time.
- The KDP select also gives you a payment for the pages that get read if you have your book on the Kindle Unlimited list. This lets people read your book for free and Amazon pays you an amount per page read. It is around 5 or 6 cents per page. Not a lot but it can add up if you have a big book and lots of people read it. There are also bonuses for the top books that are incredibly good. When you get more books and you publish them as a box set, you may not want to put them into the unlimited program. You will get lots of page reads but it may not equal the sales you will lose by letting people read it for free. Do a comparison and see.
- Next is the pricing. Most books sell for the $2.99 price point. This is where you can get the most royalties while not pricing out of the market. At $2.99 with a normal book, you will make somewhere around $2.00 in royalties per book. You can change this anytime to run specials as you see fit. I would start at launch at $.99 for the book. You will get less in royalties, but you will get more

sales and more exposure. If you start with high sales numbers. Amazon will help you sell your book by placing it where more people will see it. Remember the point of the program is for Amazon to make money. The more books you sell the more you make, and the more Amazon makes. I let the system set the pricing for other countries.
- Next is the matchbook program. This is optional, but I take part. It lets anyone who buys a hard copy of the book, buy a digital copy at a lower price. $.99 or Free. This is your choice; it is a good thing to do.
- Next is the book lending. This is also optional and up to you. People can lend the book to someone else for free for a time. If you have 70% royalties, you must allow lending.
- Read the terms and conditions and hit publish. It says it takes up to 72 hours, but most of the time my books are up for sale in less than 12 hours.
- If you change your book, you go through the same steps, change the items you want to change. It will take time to get the changes made as well. Your book is still for sale without the changes until they get the

changes made, so your book does not go away for a day or two.

Once published then comes the marketing for your book. Marketing will come in another book. Marketing is a big topic. This is the main thing you need to do to start. Get a quality book published.

LAUNCHING YOUR BOOK

When you launch your book, there are a lot of options on how you do it. The method I found that works best is below.

- If you have a mailing list, notify them ahead of time you have a new book coming out. Let them know they will be the first to know when the book will be available. If you do not have a mailing list, read up on starting one and get it going as soon as you can. It is beyond the scope of this book.
- Get your book published and up on the Amazon site with a price of $.99. Do a quick promo to get readers and try to get reviews. Reviews are important but do not break the rules for getting them. You cannot pay for them or pay people to review for you. You can give them a free or discounted copy to get a review, but do not try to beat the system. It is not worth getting your account canceled.

- After you get it up for sale, ask friends and relatives if they would read it and give you an honest review of the book. Having positive reviews before the main launch will get you more sales.
- When you are ready for the main launch day, launch the book for 3 free days with the KDP free promo offer. To do this, go to your KDP site and click on the promote button next to the book you want to promote. Select the free promo and set up the days you want to have it for free. I do 3 days on the launch. When the free promo comes off have the book be a $.99 for a week or so to generate more sales at launch. It may feel counterproductive to give it away free and then for only $.99 to start but like I said. Get the sales off to a good start. Amazon will help you in a big way with more sales and that is where you will get the best return. After the free days and a week at $.99 raise the price to the selling price you want the book at, and you are good to go.

Promoting your book after the launch is much more involved, and for another book. There are a million ways to promote your book. But if you write a quality book and launch it right, Amazon will do a lot of promoting for you and save you a ton of work.

CREATING PAPERBACKS

The next step is set up paperbacks, set up to sell physical copies of your books. You may think this is not important but your wrong. Believe it or not 50% of my book sales are from paperbacks. Not everyone wants a digital copy, and some want both paper and digital. In November and December up to 80% of my sales are paper copies.

You will create your paperbacks on Amazon where you create your digital books. November and December are fantastic months for print book sales. People buy books for gifts, and the physical copies are better for gifts.

The process for creating the paperbacks on Amazon are similar. It is easier than it was on CreateSpace.

Set up your book file in Google docs or word.
Go to page setup, set for 6 x 9 page, and set margins to .75 all around.
Go through file and make sure all photos and text are inside the page cut off.

- Set up your book title and subtitle. The title and subtitle for your paperback entry must match the cover of the book exactly. If not, you cannot finish getting it up for sale.
- Choose paperback and select guided.
- Pick a free CreateSpace ISBN or use your own if you have one.
- Pick black and white and 6 x 9. This is most common size.
- Upload your book file when you have it set up.
- Upload your cover or create a cover on the site. Follow the directions to walk you through it.
- When entering the cover. The easiest and best way is to open the cover creator and pick a style you want. Go through each step in the cover creator and enter the parts you want. Make the parts not visible if you do not want them to show. Go through each step before it will let you finish the cover. This will create a front cover, a back cover, and the spine for your book. Upload the picture you used on your book cover on KDP or change it to a different one if you want.
- Open the file reviewer and make sure the chapters all start on their own page. And that all photos are inside the borders, and that

- everything looks good. When it does you can move on to the next step.
- Follow the guide to enter the rest of the book.
-
- When you get everything entered, submit your files for approval. You will get an email most of the time within 12 to 24 hours. If something is not correct, you need to go back and fix what they say you need to fix.
- After you submit the files, you will need to pick a category. Then enter the keywords and pick your distribution. You can pick the ones you want or pick all. I pick them all for the widest distribution for sales.

Follow the guided entry and it will go smooth. After you do the first one it is much easier.
You should order at least one paperback copy of your books so you have it and can share it and promote it. I always have a copy of a couple different books I can show off.

CONCLUSION

You can write a book and publish it and do it all on your own. It takes work, and it is not a get rich quick venture. It is a rewarding and fun venture if you like to write and you want to share knowledge and help people solve their problems.

Go through the book and follow the chapters that are laid out for you. This will save you a lot of trial and error to get from the beginning to the end of the process.

If you have questions, you can contact me at Steve@stevepease.net.

Reviews for books are important in getting people to look at books. **If you could spare a couple minutes to write a review**, it would be appreciated.

Check out my website for books on Fishing, photography, exercise, Wi-Fi, and many Christian related subjects. Stevepease.net

ABOUT ME

My name is Steve Pease. I live in the Northern suburbs of the Twin Cities in Minnesota.

I have been writing for about six years. I have written several hundred articles for Hub pages and for examiner over the years. For Examiner, I wrote a column for the Twin Cities on Disc golf, and one on Cycling in the Twin Cities, and one on Exercise and fitness for the Twin cities.

I write on subjects I am passionate about, disc golf, exercise, photography, cycling, fishing, and topics that deal with Christian beliefs.

My father is a retired minister, and he has written many books. I have edited many of them and have them available on my site that cover many topics of interest to Christians today. I have also written an Old Testament trivia book on my own.

I have been playing disc golf since 1978 and love the sport.

The greatest thing about disc golf is at age sixty, I am still competitive and beat players much younger than me. Disc golf is a sport you can play at almost any age if you can walk.

I have taken several hundred thousand pictures over the last 35 years, and I am constantly trying to improve my photography. My goal is always to take the best shots I can. I want people to say wow when they look at my shots. I went through the photography course at New York Institute of photography many years ago. What I learned from the course, and my years of experience were worth every dollar.

The key to be a great photographer is to see things that most people do not see, or in a way, they did not see it.

My favorite types of photography are landscape, portrait, animals and infrared. I have shot several weddings and spend hundreds of hours just exploring different places looking for great things to take pictures of.
I have been an avid fisherman since I was a kid. I have had two bass fishing boats over the years, but I enjoy fishing for my kayak. I have a sit inside old town kayak, and a sit on top feelfree Moken 12 fishing kayak. I also have two old town canoes for going to the boundary waters canoe area wilderness area or just paddling around lakes in my area.

The hardest part about fishing from a kayak is trying to decide what not to take with me. As with most bass fishermen I have tons of equipment, and I always feel I need to take it all with me in case I need it. Kayak fishing has made me downsize just to fit everything in my kayak.

I spend most of my fishing time catching bass and northern pike. However, if I am looking for a good meal, you cannot beat crappies and sunfish. I have spent most of my time fishing freshwater, but I have caught saltwater fish. The biggest was a 380-pound bull shark off Key West Florida in 1985.

I have also loved biking and exercising since I was in my early teens. I like to read nonfiction books so I can keep learning new things all the time. Many of the things I learn I want to share with you and help enrich your life. I want to pass on the knowledge I have learned over the years and share it with others.
Thanks again

Check out my book site for other good books. Stevepease. net

Printed in Great Britain
by Amazon